SOUL WHISPERS ON PAPER

SHIVA SHALINI

BookLeaf Publishing

India | USA | UK

Presentation by *BookLeaf Publishing*

Web: www.bookleafpub.com

E-mail: info@bookleafpub.com

ISBN: 9789360948580

First edition 2024

To The Almighty, My God, who is The Creator of All.

To my Parents and family, Mrs Sangita Singh, Mr Samrendra Kumar Singh, Mrs Payal, Mr Swet Saurabh, Shivanshi (Puggi). Thank you for the constant support and my pride.

To Dr Sathwik Reddy Nandikonda, who framed my words into beautiful sentences, who made me fall in love with my own jumbled letters, whose thoughts are stolen here and are put up in an organized poetries, who inspired and encouraged me to make this possible and many more. "Thank you."

ACKNOWLEDGEMENT

I would like to thank this platform, The Publisher, for creating this opportunity.
I would like to thank my leading role in this book, The Nature.
I would like to thank all my readers. You belong to the most important ones in an author's life.

PREFACE

The phrases recorded in this book are based on real emotions. Poems belong to various contents that are listed at different times and reflect diversity in feelings. This book of poetry believes in a simple reason that you may fully grasp the content and understand the detailing. It focuses on guiding you along the walk of vehemence, power of relationships, spirit of love and meaning of romance. We come across a lot of attractions in our day-to-day life and we leave them unnoticed. My aim is simply to gather your attention and make you visualize the importance of living. There is a parallel world that has plenty of emotions, both good and worse. This world is hidden within our inner self. To enter this world, I would ask for your better time, to read and imagine. Though your imagination might take time, you will see the actual taste of reality. I am too young to understand the meaning of life and it's too early to experience the chapter of living, but despite this, my actual aim is to make you flutter in the rhymes and show you God's truth. This book will share my thoughts with no focus on judgment and you have an absolute right, the right to disagree. Precautions have been taken in order to avoid any sort of hard feelings. I apologize for any unforeseen dissatisfaction if any.

THE UNSPOKEN MATTER

MATTERS OF DESIRE
A DESIRE TO LOVE, A DESIRE TO
RECREATE

Deep down from the inner peace
I heard a voice that kept me awake
The voice vanished I had to race
In search of matter with life at stake

To my surprise found no such matter
My thoughts aligned to later define
The elucidation of love in ways of patter
This love felt pure no need to refine

The voice unspoken the voice not heard
Rose a desire with a decent attire
A zeal to love to keep it harbored
In quest to be loved and make it prior

A promise to self in search of voice
The matter unspoken the desire felt mighty
To recreate the peace to resume the voice
The love to cure as pure as the Almighty

THE MIND GAME

WE LIVE THE PRESENT WITH HOPES OF
TOMORROW
THEN ENTER IN TOMORROW WITH EYES
OF SORROW

From the world of today
I called you future once
From the dream of past
I had you for months

My memories my thoughts
Come close to unite
Did good we achieve
Help me to write

On one fine day of the beautiful summer
I made a choice the choice of hope
I lived the moment to grow stunner
Astounding was the hope
With an uphill slope

The desire I had the dream I raised
Were nowhere perceived
Had shaken my faith
Was this the future I longed and craved
What time could change past look outbraved

The day well there
Made memories conspicuous
Those memories of achievement
Those hopes were auspicious
O' Almighty my mind you played a good game
What mysteries more planned
Are those to proclaim

THE PIONEERING PROFILE

THE JOURNEY OF HOPE THE DESIRE TO
GROWTH
TO REACH MY DESTINATION I REPEAT
MY OATH

The stars from valley the moon behind hills
Aroused me from nap in mid winter chills
They created fine gestures that shook me in
thrills
Gazing on my path they questioned me what
wills

Their stagger was authentic the custody felt
relished
I knocked up to answer to sound it embellished
The journey of mine was crowned up nourished
Each time it startles what if all perished

The journey of hope the path to success
The penumbra is apparent my agony I confess
With all torment in I plump up to progress
On day quite near I will foot on to address

The address to destination is no matter to hide
Some call it dream others tag this a ride
I claim this a journey and a matter of pride
I say it out loud you will hear them gazillion
times
This is my own made path God has sent chimes

The moon the stars you cardinals of nature
Thank you the most you did me a favor
The question you raised made me a creator
The creator of belief and spirit of an achiever

MY OWN MIXED THOUGHTS

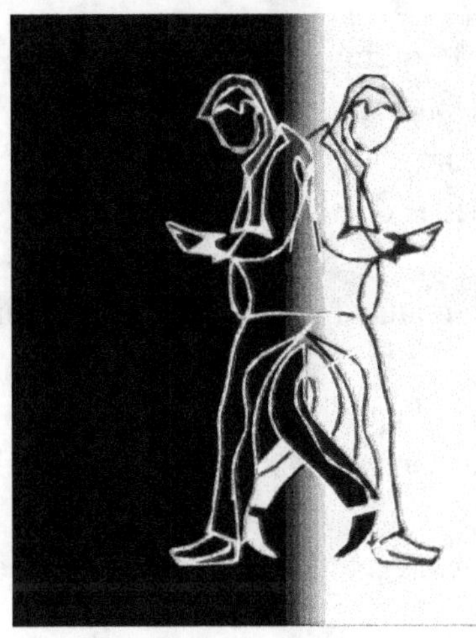

Just like my other days I was tired and about to
sleep
My eyelids were all set to relax
Suddenly there was a glimpse of an unusual
feeling
And I felt a result of uncertainty
My mind raised a question and I lost my peace

I was happy working the entire day
The success I had seen once is more near

But what kept me awake were my mixed
thoughts
When I looked back to the point of start
I was mesmerized and sank within the choices

Is it all worth to follow a single track
And leave the other sources of happiness
Am I that mature enough to secure my future
When insecurities overrule my joy of present

what could be retained was my mind struggling
between two
The two forms of emotions
At times I was happy and within seconds I felt
sad
Are those my exaggeration or their coexistence
is a rule

Lying by my side my phone starts ringing
It's 5 am and I was unable to sleep the entire
night
Those questions were unanswered and thoughts
get jumbled up
With my so-called happy face
My soul is ready and dressed up for a new day

THE REAL TIME ICEBERG: Life of a Doctor

THE WORLD YOU SEE IS A PREVUE
CREATION
THE CHARGE I HEFT IS A STEALTHY
PASSION

Sometimes when I look through the mirror
Vocation I belong to is spotted as a terror
The hidden shadow sits beneath the river
With a picture apparent as a fake shimmer

All good you believe what joy you see
Is a notion fallacious and a desire I plea
The struggle you count as two or three
Are trifling and tiny not worth the degree

For what you call I grapple to compete
You look me read as hard as a dweeb
The sympathy you give is not a treat
Come face my root covered by sheet

Some worry are intense those grief are objective
How do I disclose they serve me protective
The whimper I hide my efforts are corrective
To outcomes I know yet desiring subjective
The joy you see the success I dream
The elite the fame and personality esteem
Chained to duty the depth unseen
The happiness of freedom I wish to redeem

My work and flaws some memories of practice
Beneath my pillow they build a lattice
To spook in my dream as thorns of cactus
I just want peace and sleep gratis

The character I play and trust I grasp
From death the immortal to life I clasp
The prevue you see is a matter of flask
My truth is immense behind my mask

THE UNSEEN BEAUTY

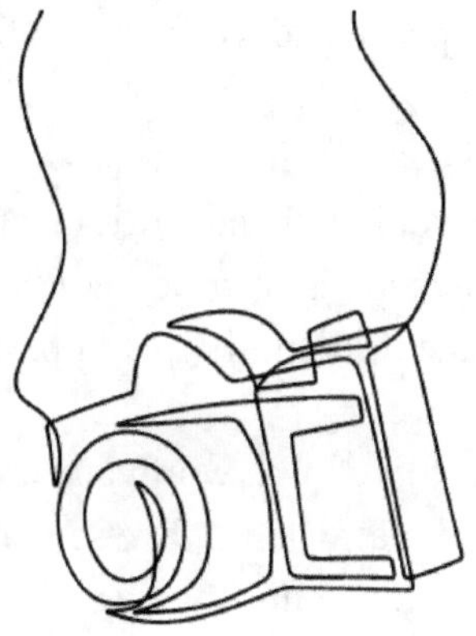

I was living in the unreal world
The world of dreams the pool of desires
Woke up to the tune, a little but musical
The globe of truth was the picture apparent

In the rush to chase I aligned my soul
Gathered up my feet with mind left in chaos
Walking through the edge was lost in the fake
Scrolls of many immersed eyes in gaze

Sudden was a slip and the phone lost my grip
By 6 in the morning with the screen turned off
What eyes could see felt heart with amaze
My journey of routine turned a fairy tale

I had no count for flowers were many
The wings of nature were so stunning
The fragrance of beauty I would love to admire
In sounds of peace and fresh air breathe

How velvety was the feel of touch
What snaps would tell and stories would define
For nature the pure and carpet of green
From moth the brittle to flights of passerine

The moment I lived was worth and angelic
Was truth and real with no fake screen
My beautiful human this message with love
I share to you in folder named clean

A small gesture from self to nature
I agree to believe is not of match
Still bow down and respect the creator
With thanks of many for a beautiful catch

THE ACTUAL STRENGTH

While climbing up in the pyramid of desire
With hopes of courage and dreams so high
I reached to tip with no left charge
And strength felt weak raised questions deep

The meaning of power and the term strength
Are those for real when read so little
Breathing on top I relaxed to believe
No more myths but elucidation

The unsaved memories from life of past
Got filmed so clear with a button of rewind
I love to share in small formed clips
And aim you to picture spread and leak

In my mid-twenties an age of seven
Reacted quiet to a puppy bite

Wrote his name in the Book of Heaven
To forgive in pain I call it strength

In a few minutes of the beautiful summer
I came across an act of kindness
While sad at life he gave me comfort
The handsome old man what courage he owned

The morning of spring with leaves on ground
From root to branches tree looked brown
A lady in gown as pretty as mermaid
Captured the site she chose to appreciate
My heart was amazed and mind in phrase
To praise is strength to admire is power

Two cute little kids down the lane
Were both in action played war as game
Where oxford serves a meaning for strong as
winner
Twin earned the trophy as one helped other

Too gentle and soft not hard nor anger
To forgive and smile no revenge and hater
These few from many are meaning and answer
For what is strength and actual power

THE MUSICAL ROMANCE

The melody in music is a form of love
Ear hits in romance with a message to brain
I get smell of talent with the taste of peace
In the process of life it gives time to heal

The strike on tabla turns pain so magical
Give voice of love so pure and lyrical
The language of violin it speaks is sensational
What I can hear is truth and vocational

The power in strings is less when define
And tuned in guitar when kept aligned
When I move my fingers in a trait of synchrony
Air dance in tune and gives me euphony

Boon to piano are black and white keys
The instrument is divine keeps mind in peace
It reflects the player and grade the performance

Read deep in mind to arrange color in
accordance

The magic in lips and link in between
When touched to flute my heart feels clean
It rubs on harmonica leaves smile unseen
To soothe the local and live in dream
The art in music is lovely and angelic
When plays in Veena sounds Godly and terrific
Are silent for words but unmixed and sterling
Offers calm to soul as lyrics come singing

Not limited to gadgets and the love is eternal
For music the supreme sounds wise and vernal
I hear them in nature too soft with clarity
And seek for their presence turns mood to
melody

The season of monsoon water down the peak
When drops in vibrance is a sound-full piece
The chirp of birds some new and familiar
Gives tune so soothing have love to deliver

The thunder and storm with wind around
And voice of drizzle under lightning's shadow
Made speech in chorus with a vivid color
Gave joy to mind and happiness shower

More forms of nature and patterns of sound
No words to describe they leave me profound
When heard it embraces The musical tenderness
I blend in romance held with gentleness

THE LONG RIDE

The decision I made was hard to believe
Through the diverse of culture and tempting
nature
Just me on my wheels and deep courage
I kept up my dream and the taste of struggle

I have a lot to share along my journey
The journey of love beyond my fear
What joy I received no money could buy
And met my strength which mind was unaware

The truth I faced is a lesson to learn
In a war of two my body and mind
I made a right choice for my body to decide
And measure my strength to fuel up my desire

What gives me comfort is a zone of restriction
The thoughts in mind give ways to claim

For not to proceed and snooze in pain
To limit my power and none to gain

About things my mind knows too little
I gave no right for them to answer
The choice to lead was firm though brittle
And body with strength said no to cripple

My way to home was of thousand miles
I rode down to travel through the chain of
cement
The connection was evident felt real of variant
Through towns of many and states were
different

The fabric of thread looked soft and familiar
Shaped in divergence from top to bottom wear
The taste of cereals was lot of variable
Flavors were added as specific to regional

I looked up to people their manners of living
It changed in a blink without any bridging
From happy kids in slum to silence in castle
And kindness in eyes to life full of hassle

My eyes were in amaze to perceive nature
The change in creation with occurrence in layer
As cold the weather to warmth in summer
To name the season was a task tougher

For days of two multiple were variations
The language and behavior reflect the education
Catch to my site was variant culture
From emotions unseen to built sculptures

My ride was long not measured in time
Felt heavy to begin finish danced in rhyme
The love for my wheels gave reason to believe
And distance of many I would love to retrieve

THE MEMORABLE ESCAPE

From my hours of 24 I escaped for minutes
I moved down for miles and came across the
vision
My eyes were mesmerized with mind in doubt
To what name as life either luxury or without

The road of flowers some tagged with castles
From aroma of love to deep in emotions
And silence in villa to kids in slum
Variance of many the fragrance to crump

My mind got mingled by path of followers
Uncovering the street from minutes to hours
When beauty to define trust eyes or mind
We modify the nature from snobbish to kind

The picture was pretty with taste of hush
while doors of jhuggi had smiles in rush
Blossom of flowers had petals to lose
And trees with stems were no more abused

To my end of escape I met one beauty
For age of 5 she was more than pretty
One rule she taught I retained for lifetime
To choose your happiness is honest with no crime

THE MESSENGER OF HOPE

THIS LOVELY FLY
WE CALL THEM BUTTERFLY

Sometimes in the middle of the day
These flying colors stepped into my way
The day passed better than the other days
Feeling nostalgic with a lot positive rays

Wafting here and there searching elsewhere
Had scattered love none can compare
Left me skeptical for real over dream
Was hard to believe as felt so clean

With passion and desire gained this attire
From moth the little to monarch but brittle
Its ride in sunshine got phrases aligned
The grapple it faced shall render a lifetime

Furthermore in the beginning of rain
When leaves were yet to be stained
Its beauty adorable that pinched my sight
Somewhere then vanished with just one flight

THE ROMANTIC PROFILE

Entangled in jam full of emotions
The meaning of love who never knew
You simplified it the best
And gave me a definite notion

Your touch gives me a sensation
Your presence has a warmth speculation
Your smell has a peculiarity
The feel comes in with clarity
When your lips touch my body
My soul sings a melody

The way you shower your feelings
Gives me strength and a reason to believe
How spiritual are those love feelings
I now know them all and do perceive

MY OLD FRIENDS

In my count of thirties I cherish to those years
The years we shared made memories for real
When I look back in time we had no fear
The happiness we lived gives evocation with
tear

The days we passed were our little lives
And wonders we made are saved and archive
The gossips in corridor to laughs on beachside
Some planned trips still await our ride

Many hours and days for I have to count
The dreams of today are tributes of account
Were those some delusion or happiness profound
From memories in picture to thoughts astound

I recall those nights we read ahead paper
Those hourly calls and never-ending
conversations
The sorrow we shared was huge and enormous
That gave us strength to raise our performance

O' Almighty your plans are prime than ours
We follow the path very distant aparts
I wish to relive those precious of hours
Old friends of mine hope never departs

THE LOVE UPTAKE

From seconds to minutes to hours and days
From phrases to books and some fairy tales
To search in for you with pain in gaze
My love so bright with lot positive rays

It gave a soft touch like a gentle breeze
In the chaos and drama i gained some relieve
Love felt like rain with the beam of light
That makes me the path and clear insight

Love comes with ease and the mental peace
Walking along the way we take steps in league
Pulled along the side like a magnetic attraction
Though obstacles of many we cleared in fraction

Love is an art a dream and an emotion
The warm embrace and a positive connection
I feel how pure is a true sensation
The color so vivid and no assumption

No terms to define less phrases to align
Your vision of reality no need be mine
My theory of destiny you sure may decline
Yet word of love is holy and divine

THE LOST SPARROW

Oh' little sparrow your thousand tales
Your wings of peace and feathers like quail
The taps on window and flutters around
And voice of chirp are nowhere found

The stripes of dark on plumage brown
How vintage the look you bird with crown
From head so tiny to dainty and round
Your glance too pretty keeps you renowned

That small height jumps and your mini feet
The voice you sing make melodious treat
From flight on trees to landing on street
Your sight was awful why fade to obsolete

My clear little bird I find you nowhere
From dusk till dawn your glimpse is so rare
The beauty of nature we need to adhere
Are lost from vision to make us aware

THAT STORMY NIGHT

One night to remember as dark as coal
I held you tight and pulled too close
The weather was fierce and spooky as a ghost
That day of fright when my life choked

The deep black clouds ran above my house
And lightning with thunder grew more than shouts
The lights on the street were flickering to sound
Were turned off in a while with a horrific bounce

The voice of wind was squeaking and thrill
Kept rattling the door and walls as drill
How branches fell off and lost the grip
The shadows were moving too fast and quick

The glass of windows was broken and shattered
And drops of rain got drizzle to scattered
How icy white bullets were scary and splattered
And the innocent animals all ran for shelter

My Almighty The God your plan was fearsome
The breath felt daunting as if locked in a prism
For survival that day was a matter of wisdom
The storm was gone I wish never come

THE SOLVED BIRTH TRAUMA: Based on real story

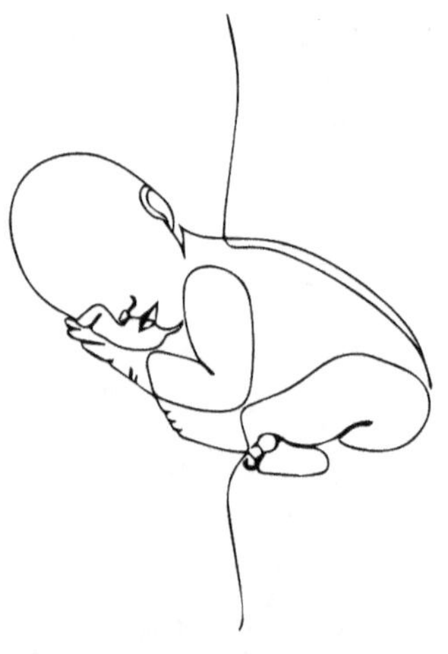

I am not a hypothetical character
I won't be narrating a fictional movie
Those miracles that day were divine
What happiness looks like was destiny of mine

That day was warm and sunny
I was all ready to be delivered
But the Almighty had some big plans
He laid me out through a narrow path
The beginning was a mistake
But what ended up is a story

In the hours of 24 I was too young to feel the
pain
And was lying peace in mother's arm
Little but not late my celebration was withheld
They called me not normal as my hand turned
pale

The white coat army was all set and ready
But there was a sense of deficiency
All prayers were heard God sent a messenger
The message for help was conveyed to my
savior
She was unaware for what changes she could do
And what outcomes she could bring
A small thought of fixing with powered desire of
success
Were ornaments to my journey and light to my
future

Yes I am normal and not called handicapped
They said change was visible from blue to pink
What I call is a marvel and a spark of inspiration
The everlasting impact got teachings for the
good
Some call it brilliant others were astonished
For what changed my life was also a lesson
Age is a number and experience is a bonus
What things of matter are your skills and passion

The volume of claps was loud and melodious
Gave no space to jealousy and no room to evil
I thank you for the miracle for revision in my
life
Your motivation for the messenger inspired him
to drive
The success and achievement are matters of
pride
I could gather my blessings with you by my side

THE DANCING FIREFLY

One summer night I walked along the lane
Twinkling stars in clear sky kept away the rain
I was happy and joyful as if no pain
When witnessed a dance the memories I contain

Thousand of glimmers left me amazed
Half up in sky rest fireflies played
The vision that night I wish have stayed
Though evocation is lasting but reality has fade

That show was noted not in a theater
For this pure and real I thank the creator
The lighting was glory with flights of beetle
And hours I stayed it raised my adrenal

With greed in demand I reached there again
To my surprise no views I could gain
This journey on repeat I would love to maintain
To see heaven on earth this location I proclaim

A LETTER TO FOREST

It was 12 in the noon I came across a story
The story of a letter from desert to the forest
Where content was pure and emotions were
deepest
Some questions were raised while some seemed
protest

Should I call jealousy or name this a grief
Where desert wants to know if they can
conceive
Are they considered ugly or it's their believe
As wrote no love to gain and they have no thieve

When on same globe why they look dull and
forests have colors
Is there a lack in grasp and they miss to pay
dolors
Why flowers and petals and diversity in cultures
Make bonds with forest with flies to flutter

While going through the letter I had a smile and
also tears
Few lines I read are worth millionaires

From birds to lions do they get shelter
Is this the reason they find you better
When you own the time and are free to answer
Send me a snap and your secrets of romancer

One matter in common we both do share
Is the blowing wind handle it with care
I am sending you appreciation with no intention
to compare
How you maintain your glory you are a winner
of sphere

THE TRUST IN TOMORROW

Every night I sleep there is a question I face
For how can I rest when left work in place
This doubt gives shiver and peace to escape
My belief in tomorrow keeps nap embrace

No assurance I will wake up after hours of doze
Yet relaxation I receive with the power of hope
The hope in the beginning and renewal of the
day
This power is generous when we wish for a
better today

In the daily routine I get too busy
The works get piled up and make me dizzy
Beyond this anxiety there is a blessing indeed
When sun shows anew I may again proceed

The darkness of night is scary to feel
But the light of moon has a boon to heal
Those hours of few get our wounds conceal
And every morning real seems better than reel

THE MIRROR TO VOICES

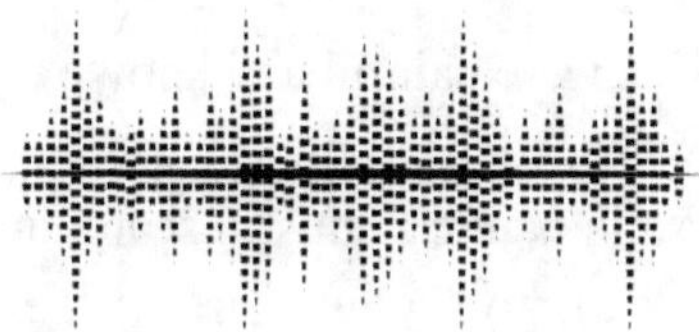

I wonder what voices meant in real
The voices of nature I heard in surreal
Their numbers are many yet few are peculiar
You must have discovered and hope are familiar

Songs were hidden in sounds of drizzle
Raindrops were happy and in a mood to giggle
Too bulk and spooky were the volume of
thunder
Seemed weep of unknown some sorrow or
plunder

A question under-covered in the voice of
animals
Were chorus and clear heard from diagonals
The echo asked reasons for why called
speechless
Are considered their sound none than worthless

The splash of water what speaks at seashore
Meanings were unclear but felt so pure

Looked deep in emotion to find a connection
The bond so real was shown in vocation

Some voices were painful and known disturbing
I sat up awakened it left me perturbing
The diverse in nature I am still searching
For me to learn my thoughts are emerging

By some words of knowledge I held up the
mirror
The mirror to voices and reality to consider
I wish you see them in depth and clear
And reveal me some more your opinions to
glitter

9 789360 948580